There is something decidedly urbane in the voice of Joan Ryan, the *sprezzatura* of courtly gestures, the *souplesse* of real silk stockings, a cheek's slight flush hidden behind a mask at a masked ball. Black swans, dark ladies, and mortals brooking dalliance with gods circumambulate the perimeter of this literary edifice, rendering the moments of self-revelation at its core all the more poignant. Delicious in their dress-up and the role-playing of myth, these poems lure the reader in with their frisson, the delivery of this daughter of the Bard: a delicious, covert code— but one, at last, that is as bracing as the face of the Magdalene illumined by light cast from a single wick.

—Lise Goett, *Leprosarium*

DARK LADIES

& OTHER AVATARS

DARK LADIES
& OTHER AVATARS

POEMS

Joan Roberta Ryan

THREE: A TAOS PRESS

Book Design & Typesetting: Lesley Cox, FEEL Design Associates, Taos, NM
Press Logo Design: William Watson, Castro Watson, New York, NY
Front Cover Artwork: Georges de la Tour, *The Repentant Magdalen*,
National Gallery of Art, Washington, D.C.
Author Photograph: Linda Cameron, Taos, NM
Text Typeset in Garamond Premier Pro

Printed in the United States of America by Cottrell Printing Company

ISBN: 978-0-9972011-6-1

THREE: A TAOS PRESS
P.O. Box 370627
Denver, CO 80237
www.3taospress.com

10 9 8 7 6 5 4 3 2 1

THREE: A TAOS PRESS

To You Who Are Not Immortal

Thank you for repairing our roof tiles
after heavy snows, pruning the lilacs in April,
installing the swamp cooler in May, keeping
the grass green in summer and the mower in gas.

By day, you remove wasp nests from rafters,
shovel walkways, trace leaky pipes
through bowels of crawlspace, build
shelves for paint cans, groceries, and books.

And by night, you epoxy cracked china,
wire my flea market lamps, keep the wood
stove burning, take out the garbage, put new ink
in my printer, retrieve Word files I lose.

For all this and the late-night feedings,
reading me Rilke, and still believing me
beautiful, I offer these poems.

Contents

TWO

THREE

One

LEDA—ON THE CHILDREN

On the other hand, the boys were easy
from the days they rode stick horses
over our courtyard, nimbling their way
through the wand weeds onto the earth
skin, chasing stray gulls, capturing crickets.

Matched as new sandals (only I could tell
Castor from Pollux, C smelling of oysters,
P of swan and blue roses), they boxed
and hunted till the verve of their play
thickened the night air to honey and the opal
moon glided like flute-song over the river.

My golden boys, my two bright stars.
On these late-winter evenings, I clasp
the lamb's wool cloak I wove for Helen
(or was it Clytemnestra?) across my shoulder
and climb this knoll to watch them shine.

PENELOPE UNRAVELED

It's the weaving that keeps her going,
guiding the wool-wrapped bobbins through sheds
of warp, making each color—Tyrian purple,
crimson kermes, blue woad, saffron, madder—
flow smoothly into the next, beating each row
into place, forming patterns she learned as a girl,
borders of chimeras, centaurs, satyrs, small
geometric figures her practiced fingers know,
listening to her women talk of lovers, lambings,
babies teething, recipes for dyes and bread.

The borders grow too fast.
For the gray-eyed goddess who lends wisdom
to her hands, she invents her own motif,
a row of the little owls that silently perch
on stone roof tiles just as daylight fades.

Unweaving is harder, slower. Nights,
she sits alone in lamp-lit silence,
picking out the hard-packed weft, its deftly
braided ends of thread and tiny hairs
that cling like wires, trying not to note
thin lines of age and darkening veins
below her bony wrists, the lessening flow
of monthly blood or how, despite steady
undoing, the shroud continues to grow.

When shadows crowd the close-walled room,
she pulls the shawl from her shoulders and steps
into the courtyard air where no slow, steady
rhythm of handwork keeps her from seeing
her husband lying cold on a thorny
hill or—as she catches a breath of white
jasmine—warm in another's bed.

SEQUEL

Dear Husband and King,
I'm writing to you because I'm afraid
someone is rewriting our story.

Lately, your mother has been
licking her lips and eyeing
the kids rather strangely,
and knowing her ogre-ish
lineage, I fear she admires
Daisy's round arms and Dawn's
dimpled knees with other
than grandmotherly affection.

I know how important your war must be,
but I'm worn out trying to make
my lamb printanier and blanquette de veau
tender enough to please her. Unless
you return to the castle with haste,
we're in imminent danger of losing,
my dear, our happily ever after.

CLYTIE AT JONES BEACH, 1961

After Ovid's Metamorphoses

Leucothoe told me he was bad news, whispered
what he did to Cyrene. And I heard about Issa
and Castalia. But I was too smart to be left in the lurch.
And he was...well—a Greek god. Into art and poetry, too.

When I walked past his stand in my almost-bikini,
he beamed down as I hoped. So I stayed till he got off duty.
Sure enough, he drops down on my blanket, picks up my book,
starts reading me Yeats, and we end up necking.

The sunburn was awful. I couldn't wear a bra
for three days. And when I got back to the beach,
he barely said *Hi*. According to Leu, someone
told him I lied about being sixteen.

Next morning, he drove by my street in his yellow MG,
Miss Someone herself sitting beside him, wearing
his varsity jacket. So I told Leu's dad how worried
I was. And that put a quick end to it.

Now he hates me, says I'm chasing him, nicknames me
Baby Fat, won't look my way—even when I cut
in front of him reading Gerard Manley Hopkins
with the dust jacket on. But I'll get him back.

I've gone two weeks already on just Tab and Saltines.
And I've promised myself by the end of next week,
my waist and my thighs will be slimmer than Leu's.

VIOLA REVISITED

I am all the daughters of my father's house,/And all the brothers, too.
— *Twelfth Night*, Act II, Scene 4

abstemious	You hold our babies gingerly as chamber pots,
prig	don't want them gurgling on your stiff white ruff,
elusive	creep soft to bed while I'm asleep, and view
aberrant	the milk stains on my bodice with disgust.
indicative	So the music's not as sweet now as before?
ambivalence	I should have listened better when you said
imminent	we are *as roses*—our flower, *once displayed,*
diminuendo	*doth fall*—and seen Viola and Olivia as cyphers
irony	for a love no sooner had than...dull routine. And if
carnal	I want you hard again between my thighs,
androgyny	I might just bind my breasts in strips of linen,
pluck	slip back into a set of hose and breeches
the illusion	and be once more your gender-bending *boy.*

Clytemnestra On Kosmetikos

Keeping up with my twin has never been easy.
For starters, sitting shrouded at noon, head
soaked in vinegar, is smelly and sweaty,
and the olive oil masque drips in my eyes—
although, as Mother reminds me,
it's a reasonable price for glossy skin and gold hair.

Even the morning soak in milk and honey
turns tedious after ten minutes, and I wince
at the thought of the scrub that must follow
with sea salt rough as coarse sand—to say nothing
of the slow, hair-by-hair plucking required
for keeping me girlish—smooth as nacre—below.

As for the make-up, I rather enjoy the art—
outlining my eyes with thin strokes of char,
brightening my lips with dabs of beetroot and beeswax
small as fig seeds, using light touches of fucus
to turn my almond complexion fairer still. And I like
the results—seven noble suitors vying for my hand.

But then there's always Helen—with nineteen
at last count and four of them kings—heedless
of politics, marriage, beauty, or fashion as she runs
off to hunt with our brothers, that full mane flying,
those long white arms and luminous
breasts bared to sunlight and wind.

WITH CRANACH, IT'S ALWAYS THE HAT

After Lucas Cranach's Cupid Complaining to Venus

The simple snood, pearl-encrusted caul,
or towering hennin, Luther's sober black beret,
the duke's velvet cap—plumed and rakishly
slanted—the merchant's fur bonnet, his wife's
tall popover—all gilt and white satin—
the widow's hood, the bishop's mitre—
each becomes, I fear, more subject than the sitter.

But for Venus, he reserves the red
velvet cartwheel rimmed in puffs
of ostrich feather. And at Frederick's court,
there was always someone fresh—long,
narrow, pippin-breasted—who'd
toss her gown behind the screen for a thaler
and happily reach for the crimson brim.

And then—*ta-dah!*—the goddess of love
more naked than nude in her hat and o
that lascivious thin Cranach smile.

ARACHNE RESTRUNG

The girl was talented indeed—scarves
you could pass through a child's
circled thumb and forefinger—
diligent, driven. And proud. I tried
to warn her. But her boasts led
to challenge and those scenes—Europa,
Danae, Leda—aimed through my father
at me. Yet I showed compassion.

Her change was sudden—
no time to dread (even consider)
the flattening of her torso's curves,
re-sectioning of arms and legs,
emergence of additional eyes
before the pain of change was over,
skin hardened into cuticle and carapace,
lips drawn into needles of chitin, thought
and dream sunk into instinct, endless
repeat. Humbling, yes, but balanced
by my gift, the mindless spinnerets;
so weaving on, she finds in patterned
craft, if not in art, her anodyne.

THREE VIEWS OF THE VENUS D'URBINO

1: In The Uffizi

Her eyes engage you as you enter the room,
equal to equal; you are the man
who holds her attention, even as you
gaze through the diagonal tease
of breast, belly and such an arm
to the uncoy hand su la figa
(she's waiting for you),
then back to curve of lip
hinting of shared pleasure.
You are the lover
she welcomes unconditionally,
the wedding chests under the window your gift,
the spaniel, Fido or Fidelia,
unawakened by its master's step.

Or, if you are a woman,
you will, as the Duke d'Urbino hoped,
become her.

2: Giulia, Her First Encounter
The too-quick Emilia unlaces
my gown. New-feathered
thoughts dart and twitter
about this unaccustomed
room, its gold and green
tapestries, dark hidden corners
where inlaid furnishings assure
me of a generous husband's care.

I look up
above the uncurtained bed,
see her lying brazen,
and stop, serpent-trapped
by that mocking glance, cannot turn away.
My mouth goes dry, stomach hollows,
nipples shrink; my body now a frightened child's,
I wonder who she is and where I've come.

3: Angela Del Moro, Courtesan

Orazio, Tiziano's son, stands at my gate again,
whistling and tossing the old man's purse.
But *no,* I say, *not still and stiff in cast-off robes*
and borrowed pearls, someone I'm not
for hours that creep at a model's pittance,
when Venetian youths bring silver
and uncles leave me gold.
Yet I miss your father's villa,
wine and capons, talk of art,
the Marys, Judiths, Ursulas I play.

Not so, Orazio fingers the pouch,
this time just you, bellissima,
with all your finery God-given.
And at a better price than Giorgione ever paid.

Well, one might do worse than show them all
of Angela del Moro, beauty undiminished;
disprove for once the spewed-up, vengeful verse—
defilement, rape, rumors of contagion—
show them why I still command
the city's highest rate. Even if I won't pretend
more pleasure than a lover gives.

I take the purse, lie
naked on the silken couch,
watch him paint, and smile that smile.
Two of a kind, Tiziano and I,
we grab the highest bidder's pay
yet never sink to compromise.

THE DARK LADY'S SONNET

The nights you wrapped my hair around your throat
and swore I brought sweet music to your life,
I gloried in each *yes* and *please* you moaned
and sucked the honeyed words you fed me dry.
More and less than friends, we swore no vows,
but bound by lust and joy, we'd faithless lie
naked on my bed on rain-swept nights, carouse,
explore—explode—as lightning cracked the London sky.

Such games you played among those seamed sheets!
Despite those *breasts of dun*, *black wires*, and *reeky breath*,
I was then your ever-changing, dark Egyptian queen,
not that apparition bleak as death,
from whose barbed grasp you longed to pull away
to pen sweet nothings for a pretty lordling's pay.

CECILIA GALLERANI

After Leonardo da Vinci's Lady with an Ermine

Beautiful, he calls her, *as a flower*
and wants her with him all ways,
finds gifts to delight her—
French passamenterie for her gown,
the velvet mantle with red-slashed sleeves,
a new viola da mano, perhaps, from Brescia—
confines her lightly as the net
holding the hair to her temples,
sheathing the luster
only he may unbraid.

He is Ludovico Sforza, *Il Moro*.
Look how she wears him about her neck—
a string of polished jet. And he is called
L'Ermilio, too—see the ermine
she caresses, fierce and priapic,
the strength of her (oversized
you think?) hands. Does she boast
she holds him, owns him, carries
his child? Who does she see in the distance?
And why does she look so sad?

Long after the indolent hours of posing,
after Sforza leaves her (before the portrait
is dry) to marry Ferrara's
pale daughter, and after Leonardo
is reassigned to engineer
the nuptial celebrations,
and after the bride dies
in childbirth, and Cecilia confides in her letter,
you would not recognize me today,
the painting—long forgotten—
is sent to Cracow where Delacroix
(who knows pourquoi?) blackens
the background, covering the window
over her shoulder, so we'll never know
what she and Leonardo saw.

BACCHINO MALATO

After Caravaggio's Self-Portrait as Bacchus

No wine, and the fruit is scant,
softening grapes to hold and
barely a bunch for the table,
peaches too hard to ripen,
and not a leaf among them.
I pull a strand of ivy through the window,
twist, and Bacchus has his crown.

I wish Minnito, sleepy-eyed,
flush-cheeked, with rounded arms,
were sitting in my place,
but even friends expect a fee—
and food and drink and laughter.

Now, for the face in the mirror.
I reach backward for the brush and wince.
The sheet about my shoulder slips;
I stop, secure it with a bell cord,
try to laugh. The lips twist up, but
the brow stays creased, and
yellowed eyes squint back in pain.

My palette needs more ochre,
terra verde, too, for flesh drawn tight,
discolored like the peaches.
The lines around the nose need darkening,
the shoulder more defining,
youth burned away.

Well, let this be the morning after,
when even godlings turn dull green.
And keep the lamp flame burning,
so my man of wealth will note
how every grape reflects the light
and draw his purse string open.

PEELING APPLES

After the painting by Pieter de Hooch

You can tell from her fur-trimmed jacket and gold-
embroidered skirt, the woman in de Hooch's painting
is not about to bake an appeltaerte.
She peels these boskoops for her daughter (see how,
eyes fixed on the blade, the girl smiles to feel
the lengthening strip glide down between her fingers)
to teach the child to peel a fruit with one long cut.

Not the fastest way, perhaps, to skin a basketful
of apples, but a skill she knows her girl will want
to master, a pretty trick to show off agile hands
and make the homely task of paring fruit intriguing
to a suitor who'll someday sit before this Delft
tile hearth and watch, an act indicative
of pride and care—this reach for form and order.

THE REPENTANT MAGDALENE

After the painting by Georges de la Tour

Silhouetted by a single candle's light,
she sits pensive like a woman
newly wakened from a dream,
right hand fingering
the cranium of one long dead
lightly as she'd touch a sleeper's brow,
left hand firmer on the petal of her cheek,
and gazes past her mirror's surface into—
we cannot see—the face of a saint or tired
girl illumined by the flame,
or just the quiet of her mind.

The canvas is her room and ours,
intimate and dark. But within the mirror's
frame, we see only the jawless skull and—
look closely, please—
the small white flame reflected in polished bone.

BREAKFAST IN EDEN

So much delights me in this garden—
as it should, since He made it for my pleasure,
to munch plump berries,
press my nose to fresh blossoms,
stroke warm fur, fleece, feathers,
and gaze at my lovely man,
my glorious giver of names.

Mornings, I wake and wonder
what new ways this day will offer
to fill our mouths with sweetness,
bathe their deep recesses
in subtle or dazzling scent.

Should I return to yesterday's branch
hung with the small purple globes
we eagerly sucked and called plums,
or reach under the gloss of these leaves
and pluck the bright suns we named oranges,
rub their firm, dimpled peels
till the oil sinks into my fingers,
then let the sharp, bright juice
slip down my throat once more?
Or shall I bite again into the flesh
of downy apricots or peaches, grainy pears—
all gifted us to taste and name?

All but from the tree He keeps for Self,
hung with only hard, dull casings,
untempting to my lips and tongue,
though smooth enough to fondle.

Or so I thought until one fell against a rock
and broke into a myriad of sparkle,
tiny gems of light and flavor
to burst against the teeth and savor—
what might it be—the taste of jewels?

Dame Van Winkle Speaks Her Mind

Others profit from his small acts of kindness,
a toy soldier whittled from a dry stick, a heavy
bucket carried home from the well. I wake
beneath a leaking roof, sit at a shaky table, turn
my daughter's dress till it can't be turned again.
And you find me sharp-tongued, shrewish, a nag,
when I call him back from the green to mend
my henyard fence or drag him from the tavern
when the last cow wanders and the wood
needs chopping before the fire dies?

I was only eighteen when I chose him, charmed
by the future I saw in his smile, his unhurried
gaze, the worlds beyond this sober valley
he opened for me with his words.

Such a web he wove with those words.
How was I to guess at twenty years
of absence, empty talk of beery dreams,
me gaunt and stooped at forty, hands
rubbed red on neighbors' soapy linens,
when I should have been dining on such cloths,
provided for by a shop or trade—perhaps
a well-run inn where folks would come
to eat my food and hear the tales
that keep me still beside him?

DARKNESS IS ANOTHER COUNTRY

Nevertheless, I saw the emperor's robes
and they were, indeed, luminous,
woven of silver, brocaded in gold
heliotropes, lions, and scatterings of finches,
with a train of purple peacocks
embroidered in pearls. And when he strode
down the palace steps, the silk cloth
flickered like the millstream waters
behind our cottage, before my eyes grew dim.

Then came the child's cry, refrained
over and over by the garrulous crowd.
And when a sober councilor quickly
swaddled our monarch in a cloak of grey
worsted, my shimmering vision was gone.

Coxcombs they called the weavers
who, sensing their peril, had already run.
But I have worn their cloth of dreams—
and if you gaze at their works and see nothing,
perhaps you are the ones who are brittle and blind.

Two

TO THE VOICES

Who are you—and why do you haunt
my sister, forbidding her to walk through the park
on Sunday, eat red berries or repeat what you say?
Why do you tell her I put drugs in her coffee
or plot to lock her out of the house?

Do you enter her padlocked rooms
through electrical outlets, radios, smoke
detectors, or speak through the television she covers
at bedtime, like the cage of a talkative parrot?
Were you ushered in through family blood,
a mutant gene or untold horror?

You have never once spoken to me. Yet
I, too, have voices. Sometimes they say
in my father's tones, *that was unworthy* or
treat her more gently. But mostly, they come
when I write, to whisper a final line
or advise me *I'd never say it this way*.
Too often, they chide me with silence.

Do you know them? Are we all related?

Close Kept

Barbara winds her way down Quesnel Street
to pick up her Marlboros and organic milk.

Muttering sotto voce, she averts
lens-shaded eyes from the horses
fenced a field-length away,
watches for cracks in the pavement
under unsteady feet, does not see me drive by.

Though tamed now by Clozaril,
the voices are with her again.
She speaks with *them* in deep private,
close guarded as the headless rubber
doll, six perfumes, and carved red bead
she seals in her triple-locked trunk.

They are people, she told me once,
but will not reveal names, ages, features
or what they say, except for the rare
they won't let me wear my turquoise earrings
or *they told me you died last night.*

I share what I know of voices—
conscience, muse, tutelary deities,
creatures who spring from the pen
with wills of their own—but she meets each probe
with only her Ginevra de' Benci stare.
Why such distrust? To whom would I reveal
her secrets, dear reader, but you?

In Hospice

I wheel my sister out to the smoking pavilion
where, withered as the Sibyl of Cumae,
she struggles to flip the top to her Marlboros,
flick her Bic and inhale. *It's t-terrible*, she coughs.
I think of the new spots on her liver, tumors growing
deep in her brain, lit-up bone scans. I wait.
Terrible, she repeats with a gurgle, then puffs
straight to the filter, while I envision
Bosch's monstrosities, Munch's *Scream*,
Breugel's *Triumph of Death* with its wagon of skulls
and charred corpses. The silence persists.
She crushes her stub on the arm of my bench.
And then, with a cloud of smoke, the utterance comes—
It's terrible not having a boyfriend.

RIP

The first choices came easy. Pink granite,
carved butterfly—best of the catalogued clichés—
and the name you owned from birth, releasing
you from *my mad sister* to someone I hardly knew.
And below? Surely not the tired generic.

But after forty-two years of up, down,
to and fro, no moment uninterrupted by trips
to the kitchen, trips to the bathroom,
coffee and toothpaste dripped on the floor,
furtive puffs, snuffing out, starting over—
the akathisia that denied you intimacy or repose—

and after seeing you, on your final night, at last lie
quiet, one arm flung behind your head, breath
slow and soft, eyes lightly closed, mouth
relaxed into almost an infant's smile, your sister
who tried for hours,
found no better line.

BARBARA IN ARIZONA

Nine days after I nest
the small walnut box of you
in the old camposanto on Las Cruces Lane,
Mother looks up from her empty lap
and asks, *Where's Barbara?*

In Arizona with Irma and Megan
(what would you have had me say?),
I lie and embroider my story as planned
with a doctor's advice for a gentler climate,
our cousins' generosity, and a six-month stay,
weaving in lunches with Scottsdale ladies,
poolside talks in striped canvas chairs
(can you see the frogs drip from my lips yet?).

Later, when your aerobics teacher calls to say
she has seen you new-risen and radiant
(don't cut me off with that thin-lipped smile),
I re-dream you in Arizona—blooming in a desert night
garden where, under the rabbit moon, you exude
white fragrance and hook fine prickles into the skin
of anyone who comes too close.

INTERPRETATION OF BARBARA

Aunt Edith, I tell my sister, *is a witch from Cuba.*
The empanada she gave you is poisoned.
I will eat it for you. She is not fooled.
And she refuses to perform in my basement review
even if I lend her the amethyst tiara—although
she's the one who dances in sync with my father's riffs
and sings on key when he plays *Stormy Weather.*

Fifty years later, she still touches her heels to her head
and does splits, but won't walk over bridges or ride
the escalator at Macy's. And she never reveals
the names of her boyfriends, why she hates cousin Irma,
or where she buried our grandmother's letters.

She is my wall of funhouse glass, silver-
smoked and unscalable, slippery minnow,
cracked opal ring, the bee in my rose of Sharon,
smell of earthworms, jellied apple, wet rubber boots,
black Mary Janes, the unnamed sepia photo—
a broken Chatty Cathy repeating, however I press,
can't tell you…can't tell you…can't tell.

ELEGY IN THE CAMPOSANTO

Time fades your image, the anger,
accusations, long silence, and I've come
to ask if you are at rest. That small
fence we built between your rose granite
stone and the neighbor's junk pile—
does the talisman-blue paint we used,
half cyan and half cerulean, keep you
safe from the voices now?

It's snowing, and by twilight, this old
Spanish cemetery where we planted you
in gaudy October will turn to silver
print. In an hour, new snow will blanket
the teddy bears and Barbies left
for lost children, tin rakes and
spades set out for gardeners.

How lightly the snow falls. How slowly
it veils grave markers and winter
stubble, plastic sunflowers and peonies,
even the spurs and sombreros—
transforming all to white offerings.

My Father's Hands

Fever gone and breath recovered, the weakness
settled in hands and feet was, they said,
Guillain-Barré; he should be grateful
to hold his cup and cut his meat.

But those were hands that guided scalpels
through men's flesh, fashioned
trout lures from bead and feather, worked
gold into bands for my mother's wrists—

and those were the hands that held
his jazz—strong, sure fingers caressing
the keys of his baby grand into ragtime or
swing, teasing long twining riffs from *Solitude*,

Mean to Me, Foggy Day, Tenderly, shift-
shaping infinite chords into ever more
intricate progressions that could wind
through a whole afternoon—

suddenly as blind to touch as if
encased in leather mitts, indifferent
to command as a dozing cat, hitting
too hard, too slow—bereft of *feel.*

A child, I knew only the silence,
the year without music, and
always those hands working
tight metal springs, hard rubber balls,

small puzzles, clay forms, presaging
notes, scales, arpeggios that would bloom
again at his fingers' touch
into blue garlands of jazz.

MOONFLOWERS

In age, my father lived in pain
and railed against an ill-tuned world.
But just before the end,
when I'd visit overnight
and the rest of us had gone to bed,
he would sit at his piano
and play into first light.

Filaments of his jazz
would wind into my room,
loop, stop, and loop again—
a few brief notes unfurled,
a breaking off...and then
the tender song
I could—no—could not place
before it bloomed into a riff,
scattered, sent out fresh shoots,
turned and counterturned,
twining under and over a melody
it teased, but never touched, until
the night and the moonflowers closed.

Ashes To Ashes

After eleven years, Dad,
I'm writing now to warn you—
Barbara's packed and ready.
She'll be arriving any day.

She seems much quieter lately—
the accusations stopped, agitation
ended, even the voices have grown silent
(may she let you rest in peace). That said,

dealing with her was never easy. In fact,
it's part of why you left. So I
feel somewhat guilty thinking
of how long she's going to stay.

But Mother said she wanted this reunion—
when such matters occupied her mind. And
asked about her wishes, Barbara cut me
off with *when you're dead, you're dead.*

DÉJÀ VU

At 93, my mother forgets where my children live
and the news from the morning *Times*, and yet,
since she came to these mountains two years ago,
finds her new world strangely familiar.

We've gone over this bridge before, she says,
the first time we drive the High Road to Mora, or
I climbed that blue gate once, many years ago.
And when we stop for lunch in Peñasco, the waitress,
or a woman at a nearby table,
will be someone she used to know.

Is a past life surfacing? Or has she seen so much
that every pattern of ridgeline and sky, barn,
fence and stream, cheekbone and smile,
floats timelessly in her mind?

PENTIMENTO

Full August, yet Mother's garden
is a sepia print on cracked parchment—
larkspur, columbine, asters,
foxgloves, all withered to *lovely flowers*—
as the magpie who scolds the dry
fountain has paled to *beautiful bird.*

Mornings, after toast and tea, she stands
at her sink picking miniscule crumbs, blind
to trellised roses inches beyond the pane,
then sits, holding her folded *Journal* where
there's *nothing much today.*
Family photos, despite the small white labels,

all have faded to *those wonderful
children* or *that sweet face.* Medications
are simply *my pills*, the dozen Seconals
she hid away at eighty, now lost in time's mist.
Still she confides at nightfall,
I am blessed.

Back To Brooklyn

At sunset, we browse through old photos,
and although she remembers little,
I am amazed by how well my mother retains
the enviable waist and firm chin of the girl
riding a rose-festooned carousel charger
at Coney Island or perched on a Prospect Park
bridge rail, smiling up at, perhaps, my father,
brushing a stray tendril back from a shoulder
behind which—at a respectable distance—
three young uniformed men smoke and observe.
And I marvel at how she still has the thick lashes
and slim legs of the Gene Tierney look-alike wheeling
my stroller past Schrafft's on Flatbush Avenue.

After I close the worn album, we look out her front
window on mountains and stars. Mother taps my shoulder—
It's time to go home. I remind her she's moved
from the house on Long Island where she spent fifty years.
But *No*, she says firmly, adjusting her skirt
over her knee, *the house on 9th Street and Avenue P,*
with yellow pansies by the stoop.

WINTER ELEGY

i

Barely a month now, and I dreamwalk
through your rooms seeking some feel
or smell of you in drawers and closets
cleared too soon, wanting to press
my face into something soft and old
worn against your skin—hoping
I missed, hooked perhaps behind
a door, a cream silk slip or your oyster-
grey alpaca shawl.

The house is too well-aired—half-used
soaps, shampoos, and caking creams
all trashed, sheets and towels fresh-
laundered. The shell that held
you, burned to ash and sealed
in a scentless hardwood box, rests
stolid on a shelf above my desk.
In June I shall carry you fifteen
hundred miles east and plant you
at my father's side.

ii

How slowly you slipped away, memory
by memory, word by word. At the end,
the names went too. All that stayed
were *lovely* and *beautiful* and, last
of all, *what should I do*? When the final
syllable left, you followed.

After you lost my name, I, too, found little
left to say, but when I brushed your hair,
you arched your neck as my young
mother did to toss away the long dark
strands that whipped her eyes on windy days.

Did we ever go out alone for a bike ride, a walk
on the beach or morning swim? What did you teach
me—other than grammar and manners, how to sew
on buttons, hem, iron, play bridge,
write sonnets and thank-you letters?
Who were you that gave me this world?
What were you thinking the night you
whispered *remorse is a terrible thing*?

iii
Over these years, so much has gone
unasked, unsaid. Or have I forgotten—
refused to see—grown beyond love?
Is this why I've heard no rustle outside
your window, no whisper, no voice in a dream?

Your leaving was so quiet, so gentle
a release on so calm a breath, it took
nothing not already lost. But now,
writing these words, I know
the silence has broken.

THREE WEEKS AFTER

Despite the piling obligations of death
certificates and thank yous, I stand
at the sink, polishing silver—a task I've
avoided for years—caught between self-
reproach and resenting the tarnish
staining my unclipped cuticles.

Yet I no sooner finish drying the art
nouveau vase I keep over the fireplace,
a Victorian cake knife last used
for your golden anniversary, and a dull-
bladed repoussé carving set, than I dash
about drawers and cabinets gathering
more favorites—the mysterious grillwork
drum with cranberry glass liner, sugar
bowl, creamer and candlesticks you received
for your wedding, and a handful of archaic
cutlery handed down from your mother.

How I coveted that olive spoon with its star-
pierced bowl, the long, skinny oyster forks
and fiercely-pronged fork for pickles
when, as a child, I'd help you remove
each piece from its grey flannel pouch once
a year, bring it back to original gleam
and repack it same day, unused.

And I delighted, years later, when you gave
them to me. Now I feel mostly guilt
for nearly ten years of ignoring
the obligation that came with these gifts.

So I polish a little harder to remove the last
stain from the cheese scoop, thinking
I do this for you—until I hear a silvery
ring as you say, *Don't be silly. Just pass
that stuff down to your granddaughters—and
rub some Oil of Olay on those hands.*

Codicil

To Catey

Let me tell you a secret about your grandmother.
The apple-blossom Limoges she's leaving you
will not be her mother's. She bought it on eBay
when your dad was too young to remember.

As for that ring she'd like passed down to your daughter,
it isn't quite a family heirloom. The art deco setting
came from Robinson Antiques on Madison Avenue;
she had the old diamond recut to fit.

And the mortar and pestle Aunt Irina brought from Odessa?
She picked it up at a yard sale, after the set she wanted
was left to her cousin Jane. She weaves these stories
in hope you'll safeguard her worldly treasures—

but also to teach you the fine art of white-
lying she learned at her own grandma's teas
where sandwiches were *buttered* with margarine
and the *Ming china cups* were back-stamped *NIPPON*.

Links To Lena (1894-1995)

rose of sharon

Lining the walk to Lena's patio. Name old as *The Song
of Songs*. Deep mauve-throated blossoms lined with bees.
Shrunken trumpets littering the path like used condoms.
My primer of beauty and pain.

gamine

Smallest girl in the photo, propped on her elbows
in a striped wool bathing suit—how it must itch
when she leaves the water. Fifteen years old with nine
brothers, she laughs through mussed hair.

inklings

Wondering when she went from Tralinsky to Trailins,
whether her father came from Russia, Poland, or Lithuania.
And this pillow I've slept on for fifty-odd years—does it
really hold down from the goose that mangled her little
finger when she toddled into her mother's henyard?

anecdotal

When the Wild West show came to Baltimore, Buffalo Bill
brought his big white stallion to her father's blacksmith
shop behind the house on Central Avenue and rode her
around the courtyard on his shoulders. *My*, she sighed
at eighty, *he was a handsome man.* And I swear on her grave,
she never read Cummings.

crepe de chine

1. Black knee-length shift covered in bugle beads, copied
by Lena from a picture she found in a 1925 *Vogue*.

2. Long triangular earrings she made me from scraps,
ten years after I wrecked the dress playing movie stars
with my sister.

ginger	How Lena's kitchen smelled on Saturday mornings when good Jewish wives should be praying in Temple.
aroma	She liked the whiff of a good cigar, could sniff out a fine Havana, smiled when Grandpa Harry smoked one—told me she rolled them as a girl in a factory.
mourning cloak	Wings of brown velvet edged in sapphire and onyx, found in the woodlands behind the dacha Lena and Harry built on Lake Peekskill. One touch, and they fall to dust.
Shalimar	Scent of Lena's evening coat and the boa with toothy fox heads—notes of bergamot, vanilla, and amber. They linger still in the brown-stained vial I found in her alligator purse.

LOST STORIES

To Molly

Before iPads and smart phones and MacBooks,
way past the day when your grandfather's
Olivetti Lettera (icon of Bauhaus modernity)
slept with dust bunnies in the crawlspace under the stairs,
even before the tempest shattered the teapot
and the dish ran away with the spoon—

when little girls with untamable voices and flyaway
thoughts—words flowing faster than ink—used
long grey feathers to write letters to grannies,
festooned *Dears, thank yous*, and *pleases* with arabesques,
indigo blots, peacock spatters and crinkles of cocoa
and learned from Masters Pete and rePete
that the descender of j is greater than the curlicue of o
but lesser by half than the loop of l,

your great, great grandmother Carrie
so longed to hold the Jade Radite, Blue Marble, or
(better still) silver filigree barrel of a *fine*
writing instrument, easy to fill and maintain portrayed
perhaps in the *Post* or *McCall's*, she (check one)
[ ] spent the week's grocery money [ ] sold
her gold braids [ ] traded her soul to see
her dark liquid thoughts race
from its reservoir, down
the gold nib.

MEMENTO MORI

Back in the day, these Barbies had power careers:
news anchor, data diva, executive, princess.
Then, after settling in with my granddaughter,
they lost their microphones, pink computers, and tiaras,
spent their prime switching outfits, rearranging hair,
primping for dates, and echoing profundities
like *Damn, I can't find my keys*.

Dismissed now, they lie about in a box, Bosch-naked,
untressed, arms twisted, legs splayed, menaced
by boys' toys—bird monster, beaked helmet-head, hare
demon, reptilian dogs, and other odd exiles.
Cast down from *The Garden of Earthly Delights*.

Three

Vanity, My Trainer

Each morning, I run by the river
with Vanity, my trainer, who sets the pace,
rushing me past bakery windows,
enticing me on with tidbits of praise.

Lithe and supple as the aspen,
tart and green as the zest of the lime,
she runs with the careless ease
of skipping stones and whistling.
Her light talk and dark coffee inspire me
till I sleep dreaming of fresh-baked bread.

By August,
my skirts will hang on concave hips,
the skin will stretch taut on my triceps
and, when the sun sinks,
I'll pull soft shawls about my shoulders
and sip chilled glasses of wine.

In October,
I shall run faster,
at times elude my trainer,
slip into a hidden path and slow to grace,
let cups of chocolate warm my fingers,
read yellowed letters in a creased leather chair.

Come December,
I'll watch brave Vanity
run past me through the slush
and barely nod her firm, sharp chin
as I raise my arm for a cab.

IN MÁLAGA

Jetlagged and sagging under the heat,
we check into our two-star hotel
and nap an exhausted two hours
before starting our secular hajj
up to the restored and graffitied battlements
of the Alcazaba and Castillo de Gibralfaro.
We gaze down on the ancient postcard city
and even more ancient sea, lost
in legend and spectacle. Taking it all in.
Oblivious.

      The wallet contained little—
a fistful of Euros, Amazon credit card
and, from our outpost of empire,
a New Mexico driver's license.
The exchange was swift and deft,
a work of art, timeless ritual reduced
to an instant. And so we made our offering
to Hermes, god of travelers and thieves.

THE TEST

~~~

Drink me, you say, and being young and thirsty, I do, in a gulp,
without reading the small print or your mother's warning glance,
liking the hints of apricot, cardamom, and seaweed, the vague metallic smell.

~~~

Name five famous Belgians.

~~~

The nosegay of fireweed, stock, and monkshood you've plucked makes my palm
tingle; a vague numbness runs up my arm. Did you know about the poison?

~~~

Crows in the April thermals whirling in gay cacophony—turn it into a haiku.

~~~

The thousand-year eggs taste of sulfur; the sea anemones might
as well be rubber; the eels, served whole, seem to swim in their broth—
we've seen small boys fish for them in sewers. Our host smiles at us with pride.

~~~

Who would you cast as King Theseus? Titania? Peter Quince?

~~~

I'm following you up Lion's Head Mountain. Four hundred feet
below the peak, I feel dizzy. Do I climb on or turn back alone?

~~~

Explain "entropy".

~~~

A large sow grunts loudly as we walk through the hotel lobby.
Our room is a cubicle with a curtain for its door.
Show me how much you want me, you whisper.

After Long Quarreling

i

When I wake to the sound of rain and the cat
nesting warm in the crook of my knees,
I lie with my face in your sleep-rumpled sheets,
peeved you've risen so early, unrepentant for last
night's words, and just to show how little I care,
drift back to sleep—until the rustle of paper
and wafts of coffee and cardamom draw me
downstairs to your offering of peace.

ii

Evenings we walk by the stream, you and I
and the old lab—lumpy, arthritic and slow.
Her hind leg trembles; yet she breaks
ice to paddle buoyant around a deep
pool and bounds back to join us
as we talk of nano-wires and e-paper
or Miranda's brave new world.
When we argue, she limps back to the car.

iii

Through the mist of the hot tub,
as garden fades to grayscale
and snow shrouds spruce and pine,
I float to your tentative hand.
Wordless, we look in at an amber-lit room
where scoured copper pans hang from vigas,
starbursts of paperwhites rise from the table,
and our small black cat peers out through the glass.

REQUEST

To my husband

And when your friend the silver-scaled
flounder next rises to your call,
say you want only our slate-roofed cottage
and time to consider subtleties of Sung prosody,
the rectification of names, campaigns of dead
emperors, why seashells fractal,
how galaxies evolve.

But tell him your wife demands
more. She needs to indulge her taste
for baby eels braised in garlic, Muscovy
duck breast with pomegranate and pine nuts,
gamey elk steak and earthy morels
served on salvers of filigreed china
in a lakeside pavilion of cinnabar and teak.
Then she wishes to sleep on eiderdown
cushions, topped by coverlets of saffron
charmeuse embroidered with poppies and scented
with attar of Damascene rose. And there she will dream
of the fisherman's hut where, barely nineteen,
she first lay with you.

TWO-STEP NIGHT

After the fairy tale Twelve Dancing Princesses

My leather cowboy boots feel
like satin slippers. The dim room
softens my crows' feet, the grooves
of your smile. And your right hand
sends me into a double-spin, back
to the nights I followed my older sisters
down stone steps through arcades
of silver elm and golden linden.

He was invisible then, beneath his cloak. But
I sensed him following me through the trees
to the dock, heard him pluck a jeweled leaf, felt
his weight shift the skiff as I was rowed to the castle,
and—o—the swift stir of air that made the lantern flames
leap each time he waltzed past on the lakeside pavilion.

By three, our satin shoes were danced
to pieces, and we were ferried back
home to our twelve narrow beds.
If we'd had boots like these, who knows
where it might have ended—the little boats
and pretty lights, the man I felt but could
not see, those ripples in the water?

TRYST

The pedicabs have long been banished
from the streets of Taipei where they wove
through the din of markets, the honk
of trucks and creak of oxcarts,
blocked the bloated sedans of generals,
vied with taxis for right of way.

But at night in monsoon season,
the air—fresh-washed
by five o'clock rains—
carries me back to a dark
curtained cab winding its way
over arched bridges
down narrow byways
past clinking blades of the knife
sharpener, the wooden clacker of the sweet
potato man, the bamboo flute of the blind masseur
to the shoji-screened house,
where silk slippers with red dragons
wait inside the door.

PODOPHILIA

Your feet, my fairy godmother
told me, *will be your fortune.*
And she taught me to perfume
them with lavender and hyssop,
sleep in socklets filled with goose
fat, rub my heels with pumice,
and buff my nails to a pearly gleam.

Under her orders, I traced
and retraced my name in the ashes
with the heel of my wooden shoe,
and I sat by the millpond daily,
teaching my toes to form
silvery heart-shaped whorls, lift
dragonflies from the surface, and dart
like pink minnows below.
By September, when
the royal invitation arrived,
I could trap small trout
with my arches and
massage them so gently,
they'd wriggle with pleasure.

The shoes, too, were my godmother's
design—Austrian crystal with four-inch
heels and a sparkle that drew
the royal gaze straight to my size 5 feet.
I left one just as she told me
in the center of the palace steps

and fled. As the world knows well,
his highness followed, slid my foot
into my slipper and claimed me as his bride.
But the storybooks never mention
the press of his lips to my instep,
my toes' long journey up his thigh, or the moans
my practiced arches evoked.

Ripe

This morning, the canyon's
aflutter with gold-checked fritillaries
coupling on ragwort and asters.
Black and white admirals
court in midair, while solitary
swallowtails seek new partners
at every stream crossing, and
small silver blues mate on each
stalk of Queen Anne's lace.
Fireweed, phlox, and wild geranium
flaunt bright pistils and carpels.

And at the base of the meadow,
a black-haired boy steps from a Caravaggio
painting, extending his hand
to the girl with wild strawberry
stains on her blue cotton skirt.

ANOSMIA

The morning coffee you brew me tastes
bitter, yet weak as warm water.
Cutting armloads of lilac, I no longer feel
your sun-warmed arm on a swing
in Amagansett or your hand in my hair.
I eat ravenously at first, but even your lamb
tagine lacks flavor, and chocolate
remains a sterile obsession.

In August, when raspberries we pick burst
in my fingers, I wipe up the juices with tissues.
Pressed to your chest in the evening,
all I long for is sleep.

The diagnosis: anosmia; prognosis:
unclear. Wait and see.
Through an autumn when you find me
weeping in smoky rooms, breads
burned, soups dry and blackened.
Through Christmas, too, when scentless
boughs shed dry needles on the rugs,
and wine by the fire is mere charade.

And then? Before the last snow, a whiff
of white onion, a green hint of dill, promising
a miracle, rebirth of memory, joy, and desire
building until I put my face to the worn shirt
you've left on our bed and, o, the rush of it,
want you hard.

Sunday Dilemma

In the high, sunlit meadows,
saffron-bright chanterelles
scent the air with apricot, pumpkin—
baby toes barely emerging from leaf
mulch and full blown gold
trumpets, ready to hand-coax
from duff beds or edge with small
blades from clefts in the shale—
girolles, pfifferlings, capo gallos,
lisichkas, peppery and fruity,
waiting just for this moment
to wipe with damp cloths
and sauté in sweet butter,
a last taste of summer.

Lower down where boughs
close over the lake trails,
porcini are popping
at the bases of white spruce,
lodged where the roots start,
peeking out from small rocks
blanketed with spruce needles,
bedded in sod—fat little
piglets lifting their heads
among dead leaves, bark
shavings, bitter browns,
and witch's hats.

From a dense world
of round growth and wood
color, they call me by glints of raw
umber, rock shape and earth
odor, virile and redolent,
king boletes to dry
and flavor our winter.

So how can I choose, love,
between the dark of the forest
and the light breaking through?

OLD PERFUMES

The old fragrances have changed or vanished,
given way to scents that breathe synthetic dreams
or hang more densely on a single note,
vanilla, amber, rose, or bergamot.

Notes too rare, dear, or toxic now are banished,
moss-hung pools turned to clearer streams.
Potpourris with powdery trails must be reblended,
ancient gardens pruned, clipped, and tended.

Yet, in old glass-stopped bottles, memories of Spanish
shawls and fox furs, silk stockings with dark seams,
young aunts' bare white shoulders draped in pale chiffon,
—the faint sillage of antique evenings—linger on.

Quelques Fleurs…Jolie Madame…Emeraude…Calèche…
Chamade…Tabu…Je Reviens…Antilope…Mon Peche.

Dear Reader,

In these fourteen lines, I promise to show you
a simple trick for losing fifteen pounds
between Thanksgiving and Valentine's Day,
without painful exercise or giving up chocolate.

I will let you in on a common herb
better than Botox at erasing deep lines
from your cheeks and forehead, and the OTC pill
that makes you the best he'll ever have.

I'll give you the maps to Bluebeard's treasure,
El Dorado and the fountain of youth,
teach you a formula for beating the market,
how to summon a genie and spin straw into gold.

Send no money now. Just lend me your trust,
despite the old rhythms of promise and pain.

THE POET BUYS HER GRANDSON A GIFT

The video game he wants is too violent
and $60 is simply absurd for a polyester
jersey stenciled *Madrid Real.*
Why not, my son-in-law offers,
buy him that new book about sharks?
So after lunch with my sister at Prune,
I swing by McNally Jackson where
a young Jude Law points me
to *Nature and Science—New Titles.*

After skimming the blurbs and preface,
I start to reach for my Visa, but stop
and reopen at random to *Mating,*
where cruising bands of young males
take turns at a solitary female
held in place by sex organs called
claspers (once in, they expand like umbrellas)
and five rows of dagger-sharp teeth. Three pages
later, intrauterine cannibalism
and a narrow escape from mom's jaws
make *Mortal Kombat* seem tasteful.
With a wistful last glance at the clerk,
I redrape my scarf and leave.

In the cab, I take out my iPad,
google *kids' soccer shirts*, and feel
a half-forgotten frisson as I picture
Iker Casillas' tanned forearms and
Christiano Ronaldo's thighs.

REDD HEDE

To Lila

At night, I plait Lila's hair,
wet and the color of damp earth
here in the Sangre de Cristos.
In the morning, as she combs it out,
Botticelli's Venus rises, and Flora
steps out from her wall in Pompeii.

Where does it come from, this pheomelanin—
source of our granddaughter's Pre-Raphaelite glory?
We review family histories, find
chestnut, walnut and honey, even
one strawberry, but no copper or auburn
gleams through our memories.

Your science books say
recessive genes for red hair
can hide in our sixteenth chromosome
awaiting their perfect mates
for countless generations. And with pride
of authorship, you point to an altar boy
father from Cork, half-Scottish mother.

But I, from an older tribe, claim
glints of red in my father's sideburns
and a faint russet haze in polaroids
of my four-year-old self as evidence
of distant descent from the House of Jesse—
children of children of David,
ruddy and beautiful of countenance.

In Barcelona

Just as they'd emptied
their third glasses of Cava
and mopped up the sauce from
the anguilas in garlic,
he licked the last drop off
her little finger and passed her
the tissue-wrapped
box of rose gold hoops
from Moska's.

And after the waiter crumbed
the table and cleared
the bottle, before
the figs and cheese,
she blushed her way
back from the damas and
handed him under the table
a small damp ball
of black silk.

PAST MERIDIAN

When I saw you first,
my fiery boy, I craved
you for your iron
thighs, that steady
heart and honest gaze.
But now that we've survived
five decades of life's mire,
and those shanks have shrunk
to fit within my aging
compass of desire, I far prefer
a tender lie, a crooked
leer, your calculated
wicked ways.

While distended we may be—
and wrinkled too—we hang
together on our vine, and
as every oenophile knows,
raisins make a fine rich wine.

If at forty, amours shrink,
what, at sixty, shall I say
to you who still outride
me through the night,
on this bright winter
morning after?

WAIT TILL THE RAIN STOPS

Don't go yet. Storms in this valley are brief.
And I need to see where you planted the garlic,
the lilies, and key to the safe, how to open
the fireplace damper and shut the flue in spring.

Tell me again about the ride to Mycenae, the sidecar
and donkey, the girl in the artichoke cart, the thin white
scar on your eyebrow, and the rest of the marionette's
tale you started the night we slept on the beach.

It's early. And the road through the gorge is slick.
So let me bring out the goat cheese and olives, the last
of the rosemary bread—and that bottle of Nuits-
Saint-Georges we brought back from Beaune in November.

Don't go yet—while so much remains untold. Stay
at least till the rain ends and what happens next unfolds.

Notes On The Poems

Cranach's *Cupid Complaining to Venus*, The National Gallery, London

Titian's *Venus d'Urbino*, Uffizi Gallery, Florence

Leonardo's *Lady with an Ermine*, Uffizi Gallery, Florence

Caravaggio's *Bacchino Malato*, Galleria Borghese, Rome

De Hooch's *Peeling Apples*, Wallace Collection, London

De La Tour's *The Repentant Magdalen*, National Gallery of Art, Washington, D.C.

akathisia: a movement disorder characterized by compulsive restlessness and anxiety

podophilia: foot fetishism

anosmia: loss of the sense of smell

sillage: the wake of a boat or the part of a fragrance that lingers in the air after a woman passes by

ACKNOWLEDGMENTS

The author wishes to thank the editors of the following publications in which these poems, some of which have been revised, originally appeared:

Assisi Journal: "The Dark Lady's Sonnet"

Atlanta Review: "Vanity, My Trainer," "Request," "Elegy In The Camposanto," "Wait Till The Rain Stops," "Cecilia Gallerani"

Calyx: "Memento Mori"

The Cape Rock: "Anosmia"

Cold Mountain Review: "Ripe"

Concho River Review: "Dear Reader"

Crab Orchard Review: "Close Kept"

Naugatuck River Review: "Penelope Unraveled"

Nimrod International Journal: "Sequel," "The Repentant Magdalene"

Off the Coast: "Bacchino Malato," "Codicil"

Prick of the Spindle: "Moonflowers," "Tryst"

Roanoke Review: "Déjà Vu," "Redd Hede," "Sunday Dilemma"

The Sow's Ear Poetry Review: "Clytie At Jones Beach," "Clytemnestra On Kosmetikos," "With Cranach, It's Always The Hat"

Spillway: "In Hospice"

Taos Journal of International Poetry and Art: "In Barcelona"

ABOUT THE AUTHOR

Joan Roberta Ryan lives in Taos, New Mexico where she indulges her passions for skiing, hiking, mushroom hunting, Mediterranean cooking—and above all— reading and writing poetry. Her poems have appeared in *Atlanta Review, Nimrod, The Sow's Ear Poetry Review, Spillway, Naugatuck River Review, Ekphrasis, Roanoke Review, Calyx, Cold Mountain Review, Off the Coast, Crab Orchard Review, Taos Journal of International Poetry and Art*, and other journals. She is the poetry editor at *Vasari21*.

Before moving to Taos in 2009, Joan headed her own direct marketing studio where she created magalogs, commercials, and direct mail packages for clients ranging from Dow Jones to Lenox Collections to AOL to Rodale Press.

Also By 3: A Taos Press

Collecting Life: Poets on Objects Known and Imagined — Madelyn Garner and Andrea Watson

Seven — Sheryl Luna

The Luminosity — Bonnie Rose Marcus

Trembling in the Bones: A Commemorative Edition — Eleanor Swanson

3 A.M. — Phyllis Hotch

Ears of Corn: Listen — Max Early

Elemental — Bill Brown

Rootwork — Veronica Golos

Farolito — Karen S. Córdova

Godwit — Eva Hooker

The Ledgerbook — William S. Barnes

The Mistress — Catherine Strisik

Library Of Small Happiness — Leslie Ullman

Day of Clean Brightness — Jane Lin

Bloodline — Radha Marcum

Hum of Our Blood — Madelyn Garner